Animals in My World

ANIMALS OF THE JUNGLE

Shelby Moran

HABA®

PowerKiDS press.

NEW YORK

Published in 2018 by The Rosen Publishing Group, Inc.
29 East 21st Street, New York, NY 10010

First Edition

Editor: Melissa Raé Shofner
Book Design: Michael Flynn

Photo Credits: Cover ecephotography/Shutterstock.com; p. 5 David Havel/Shutterstock.com; p. 6 KobchaiMa/Shutterstock.com; p. 9 Morris Mann/Shutterstock.com; pp. 10, 24 (bill) Filipe Frazao/Shutterstock.com; pp. 13, 24 (leaves) Miami2you/Shutterstock.com; p. 14 Aleksey Stemmer/Shutterstock.com; p. 17 leisuretime70/Shutterstock.com; p. 18 ANDRE DIB/Shutterstock.com; pp. 21, 24 (tail) Pavel Kovacs/Shutterstock.com; p. 22 kungverylucky/Shutterstock.com.

Cataloging-in-Publication Data

Names: Moran, Shelby.
Title: Animals of the jungle / Shelby Moran.
Description: New York : PowerKids Press, 2018. | Series: Animals in my world | Includes index.
Identifiers: ISBN 9781538321409 (pbk.) | ISBN 9781538321423 (library bound) | ISBN 9781538321416 (6 pack)
Subjects: LCSH: Jungle animals–Juvenile literature.
Classification: LCC QL112.M67 2018 | DDC 591.73–dc23

Manufactured in the United States of America

CPSIA Compliance Information: Batch #BS17PK: For Further Information contact Rosen Publishing, New York, New York at 1-800-237-9932

Please visit: www.rosenpublishing.com and www.habausa.com

CONTENTS

Jungle Animals

Many animals live in the jungle. Some live in trees. Others live in water. Jungle animals come in all shapes and sizes. They're often very colorful.

Reptiles

Crocodiles have a long snout. Their teeth are sharp and pointy. Crocodiles love to swim. They have short legs so they can't run very fast. Crocodiles like to lie in the sun.

Pythons are snakes. Some are bright green. They're long and thin. Pythons move along the ground. They also hide in trees. Pythons swallow their food whole.

Birds

Toucans are colorful birds! They have a big bill. It helps them grab fruit and bugs. They eat frogs and eggs, too. Their wings are big. They live high up in trees.

Parrots have bright feathers. They are red, blue, green, and yellow. Parrots eat bugs and fruit. Parrots are very smart. They can learn to talk. Some can be very loud!

Amphibians

Tree frogs are bright green. Their feet are sticky, and they're great at climbing trees. Tree frogs eat bugs! They sit in the sun all day and move around at night.

Mammals

Tapirs are black and white. They have a funny nose. They eat fruit and leaves. Tapirs love the water. They swim and dive. They sleep during the day and play at night!

Jaguars have lots of spots! They are orange and black. Jaguars run fast and have sharp teeth. They have sharp claws, too. Jaguars love to play in the water.

Lemurs live in trees. They jump and climb. Their long tails help them balance. Lemurs eat fruit, leaves, and bugs. They love to be with their friends.

Sloths live in trees. They have long claws. They hang upside down. Sloths move so slowly that plants sometimes grow on them! They eat leaves and fruit.

WORDS TO KNOW

bill

leaves

tail

INDEX